Words of Life Vol. III: Works of Christian Poetry

by Patrick Henry

All Scripture quotations, unless otherwise stated, are from the King James Version of The Bible.

Cover Design: Raw Designz Studios

3P: PH Pentecostal Publishing, LLC
New Albany, OH
3p-phpentecostalpublishing.weebly.com

In Memoriam

To my father in the Gospel,
Bishop Dr. D. Rayford Bell, Ph.D., Th.D.,
who did so much to shape my spirituality
in a positive manner.

To my dear brother, Deacon Coats,
I'm glad I got to know you
before you went home.
I'll do O'Charley's in remembrance of you!

To my sweet sister, Goose,
I see you in Angelique's face.
You're ever in my heart.

To Ti Cho, my beloved grandpa
I wish you got to see Cat & ZJ grow up.
You're gone but not forgotten.

To Monman Rouge, my sweet grandma
I will never forget our first meeting,
and I hope to see you again.

Contents

Preface
God In Me & Me In God

In the Apostolic movement, saints typically emphasize the spiritual reality that God lives within us through His Holy Spirit. While this is evident, it must also be noted that we (saints) are also in God (see John 17:21 & I Corinthians 8:6)! This highlights the theme of this third volume of Christian poetry: God is in me and I am in God. Furthermore, God is in every saint, and all saints are one in God.

The image on this book's cover effectively expounds upon this theme in a vivid and efficient manner. Each facet of the image conveys deep meaning and underscores the theme of this volume. Two pivotal questions must be answered. First, how can an infinite God reside within us, who are finite beings? Second, how can we, as physical creatures, reside within God Who is a spirit (see John 4:24)?

Let's address the first question and how the cover image expresses the answer to it. Saints have the abiding presence of the Holy Spirit within their mortal body. This experience equates to being born of the Spirit, and is taught by Jesus in John 3:3-8. In order to receive the indwelling of the Holy Spirit, one must simply repent of their sins, as taught by Peter in Acts 2:38. Repentance is being deeply sorry to God for offending Him, so much so that you desire to cease offending Him via your habitual sin.

According to Proverbs 20:27, mankind was created with a human spirit. This is distinct from, yet related to, the Holy Spirit, as the Holy Spirit is the Spirit of God. Once an individual is born again or born from above according to John 3:5 and Acts 2:38, this person now has a new, indwelling, divine spirit that now is linked to the Holy Spirit.

The best conceptualization of this is brought to us in Mark 2:22. Here, Jesus teaches that the indwelling of His Spirit within our spirit can be likened to the placing of new wine into new wineskins (containers). Furthermore, He declares that it is illogical to place new wine into old wineskins, for the new wine will destroy the old wineskins! Therefore, we can deduce that when a person repents, God first gives them a new, supernatural spirit (new wine skins), and then fills this spirit with the Holy Spirit (new wine). He must do this because His infinite essence could not possibly be contained by our fallen human spirit; thus, it must be replaced. One's old human spirit is replaced with this new supernatural spirit. The new supernatural spirit is now connected intimately to the Holy Spirit, such that this divine spirit can serve as a conduit through which the soul can be transformed daily by the Holy Spirit. This reality is represented graphically on the cover of this book through the image of the man with the wine and wineskin inside of him.

This brings us to the second question: how can we reside in God? Let us once again turn to the Scriptures for clarity. I Corinthians 8:6 and John 17:21 teach us that the saints of God are one *in* God. How can this be? This reality is a spiritual reality. In other words, spiritually-speaking, all saints are one in God. As His children we are members of His Body; we are positioned, spiritually, in Him (see Ephesians 2:6).

This is represented graphically through the backdrop against which the man is set; this backdrop represents God. First, the backdrop is white which signifies the purity and holiness of God. Second, the backdrop has three infinity symbols, which represent God's infinite nature and the Godhead. (The Godhead is the reality that the One True God manifests Himself to man as Father, Son, and Holy Spirit for the purposes of reconciliation and relationship. There is but One God Who reveals Himself in these three manifestations.) Finally, each infinity symbol has stars and planets within them; this alludes to the fact that all of creation - even the entire universe - is the handiwork of God.

Therefore, in this volume, I share my ruminations concerning God and the ramifications of Him living within me. I explore these supernatural realities in both free verse and rhyme, poetry and song. In the process, I examine the two foci of these ruminations: God and me.

Incidentally, you will notice Bible verses at the beginning of certain poems. I do this to offer a way to introduce the poem. Thus, before reading a poem with such an introduction it might help to look up the Bible verse(s) mentioned prior to a particular poem in order to gain a deeper understanding of the poem. Similarly, you will notice, Bible verses to the right of particular lines of some poems; these Bible verses are meant to provide a Scriptural basis for the main point of the particular line of poetry with which it is paired. Also, in Part II where I use the term "you" consider it God literally speaking to me and every born again, tongue-talking, water baptized Christian, as we are all one in Christ. Finally, you will notice that this third volume has 33 poems (excluding the prologue); 33 represents each year of Jesus' life on earth. I hope you are edified by reading these words and all the poems that follow!

God Bless You & Yours,

Minister Patrick Henry, M.A., M.A., LPC

Prologue:

<u>My Hope For Poetry</u>

i write

words
wonderful words
wrought within

recollections
reminiscent of
winters & warm-seasons
once were, once-again

one writes words remarking upon
weeks-gone
weeks-now
weeks-next
ringing of revelations remarkable...
one-Lord oneness
one-Faith
one-Baptism
one-Love
one-Salvation won...derful

when Jesus relates words,

i write

Part I:

ALL ABOUT JESUS

JESUS Is…

Lamb of God (John 1:36)
Lion of the tribe of Judah (Revelation 5:5)
the Holy One and the Just (Acts 3:14)
Shepherd and Bishop of your souls (I Peter 2:25)
captain of their salvation (Hebrews 2:10)
great high priest (Hebrews 4:14)
door of the sheep (John 10:7)
the way, the truth, and the life (John 14:6)
Prince of life (Acts 3:15)
advocate with the Father (I John 2:1)
Wonderful (Isaiah 9:6)
Prince of Peace (Isaiah 9:6)
I AM THAT I AM (Exodus 3:14)
Immanuel (Isaiah 7:14)
faithful witness (Revelation 1:5)
good shepherd (John 10:11)
bread of life (John 6:35)
living water (John 4:10-14)
love (I John 4:8)
heir of all things (Hebrews 1:2)
the Almighty (Revelation 1:8)
Ancient of days (Daniel 7:9)
Holy One of Israel (II Kings 19:22)
Counselor (Isaiah 9:6)
light of the world (John 8:12)
resurrection and the life (John 11:25)
true vine (John 15:1)
man of sorrows (Isaiah 53:3)
everlasting Father (Isaiah 9:6)
author and finisher of our faith (Hebrews 12:2)

Branch (Isaiah 11:1)
root and offspring of David (Revelation 22:16;
Revelation 5:5)
The Word of God (Revelation 19:13)
Faithful and True (Revelation 19:11)
Sun of righteousness (Malachi 4:2)
mediator of a better covenant (Hebrews 8:6)
the Lord, which is, and which was, and which is to
come (Revelation 1:8)
Jehovah-jireh (Genesis 22:14)
Jehovah-nissi (Exodus 17:15)
Jehovah-shalom (Judges 6:23-24)
Jehovah-tsidkenu (Jeremiah 23:6)
Jehovah-rapha (Exodus 15:26)
Jehovah-shammah (Ezekiel 48:35)
Jehovah-raah (Psalm 23:1)
Alpha and Omega (Revelation 1:8)
the beginning and the end (Revelation 22:13)
the bright and morning star (Revelation 22:16)
Apostle and High Priest of our profession (Hebrews 3:1)
the only Potentate (I Timothy 6:15)
Son of man (Matthew 8:20)
King of kings and Lord of lords (Revelation 19:16)
Son of God…In other words, (Matthew 16:16)
Jesus is God. (Isaiah 9:6, I John 5:20; John 10:30)

Touch The Mystery, (Continued)
I Timothy 3:16

Hands small enough to fit on a cross
yet large enough to carry all problems
soft enough to cradle my heart
skilled enough to orchestrate HIStory

A face that's common, calm, and comely
We made it undesirable
yet, wearing a smile belying wondrous warmth
a countenance brighter than the sun

Eyes, tearful from distance with the Father
yet ablaze with zeal for Him
viewing both the start and end at once
peering into prideful hearts, and the depths of our
souls

Arms fragile enough to seize from pain and shock
as they stretched on a tree
yet wide enough to overshadow all willing
and strong enough to save

A heart that broke when Jews rejected it
while it pumped blood the same as ours,
yet it is unlike any other blood
for it bought our healing, protects us, cleanses us

A body that looks like mine
yet housing a brain fit for omniscience,
power without limit or cessation,

yet bereft of the sin-factor.

A soul that had to learn its body
whose desire for God burned like the sun
whose will was to finish God's work
whose mind exceeded any in brilliance

A spirit that transcends humble
as Your glory You disrobed
trading crowns for thorns
and luminary radiance for rags

All this and more:
the manly and the mighty
the human and the heavenly
the earthly and the eternal
woven together in a timeless tapestry

Perfection personified
Defying description and
Beyond understanding

Thus, we must receive Him
In order to...

Touch the Mystery

Be Exalted
A Psalm of Praise
Psalm 108:5

Verse 1
We raise one voice
To testify of You
You are our choice
Be magnified in our view

Verse 2
We raise one voice
To sing Your praise
Let all creation rejoice
Our hands we raise

Chorus
Be exalted in heaven
Be exalted in the earth
In You there's no leaven
None can measure Your worth

Bridge
Jesus, You are infinite
Your glory exceeds all
We bow our will to Yours
Now our problems seem small
For You transcend
The heavens, earth, & universe
Be manifested in them
Prove the truth of every verse
With the fruit of our lips
We lift You up high

That all the sons of men
You might draw nigh

Chorus
Be exalted in heaven
Be exalted in the earth
In You there's no leaven
None can measure Your worth

Be exalted
Be exalted
Be exalted
Be exalted
Be exalted

You are our choice
Be magnified in our view

Before The Beginning
Genesis 1:1

In the beginning
God created…

But what was before this?
Before the heavens & the earth
before He awakened man with a kiss
of His breath?

Before the sun
gave its light
reflected by the moon
which governs the night

Before all things,
created or made,
was an uncreated realm
in which there's no shade

For the 1st Mover
always lives, always has, always will
In this realm of Light He resides
yet manifests in ours, what a thrill!

Indeed, God transcends
the work of His hands
Before His Word made anything
there was only One. Man!
Before the beginning.

The Non-Created Christ

John 1:1-3; Colossians 1:16-17; Hebrews 1:3; I
Timothy 3:16

ALL things were made,
are made,
will be made,
except the One
ALL things,
Except the Christ…
space,
time,
heaven,
gravity,
angels,
orbits,
sun, moon, and stars
indeed, the universe,
ALL were created
by and for Christ

Yet He is non-created
For the One has always been
And always will be
Therefore, He is I AM
For as Creator
He transcends all created things
Even reality itself

This Christ
Holds all creation together
In Himself &
By His rhema Word

Although He was born of Mary
Yet, birth merely manifested Him
In the material realm
For He alone is eternal:
the I AM

The One is He
He is God &
God is Jesus of Nazareth:
The non-created Christ

Cross/Words, Part II

A Psalm of Worship

Chorus
Though your sins seem so tall
In love He earnestly calls
Jesus desires none to fall
His cross/words aren't cross at all

Verse 1
His cross speaks, "healing."
His cross speaks, "hope."
His cross speaks, "reconcile."
His cross speaks, "cope."

Bridge
Trying to earn heaven by works?
Come!
Cannot speak because of hurts?
Come!
Fearful of him who lurks?
Come!

There's room at His cross for you
There's room at His cross for you
There's room at His cross for you
There's room at His cross for you
There's room at His cross for you

Chorus
Though your sins seem so tall
In love He earnestly calls
Jesus desires none to fall

No child, His cross/words aren't cross at all

Intelligence Personified
I Corinthians 1:30

If intelligence was a person,
He would be You:
beyond wonderfully made
of a heavenly hue

If intelligence was a person,
He created all at thought-speed
speaking few words
to make complex realities

If intelligence was a person,
He would know it all:
from the exact breadth of the universe
to the subatomic, so small

If intelligence was a person,
His imprint would mark all existence.
now, we cannot fully know it
despite our intent and persistence.

If intelligence was a person,
His wisdom would be written
in all His handiwork
in plain sight, yet hidden.

If intelligence was a person,
His imagination looses within us hope
fueling our supernatural resilience
striving for better within our scope

If intelligence was a person
Knowledge is His home
Understanding is His blueprint
both transcend where my mind may roam…

In this life, this can't be denied:
Jesus is intelligence personified!

KING Of Kings
Revelation 19:16

You reign supreme
Over all kings
For You made them all
Affording them fleeting power

For their reigns must end
While Yours extends into eternity
Over the throne of David
You sit, high & exalted

The sceptre will never depart
From Your loving grasp
Which gently gathers Your friends
Your foes die twice without mercy

While transitory kings
Have domains with limits
Your jurisdiction: all creation
And all therein

While human kings
Are subject to faulty morals
You judge righteously
Meting out decrees fairly

While only one's subjects
Bow to earthly kings
ALL will bow to You one day...

But I do not wait
Rather I bow *now*
And kiss the ring of the
KING of Kings:
Jesus Christ

The Giver
John 3:16; James 1:17

You gave Your life,
yes, You did.
You gave Your life.
This fact isn't hid.

You gave Your Son,
what a sacrifice!
You gave Your Son.
His Passion wasn't nice.

You gave us Your Spirit,
Your power within.
You gave us Your Spirit,
that we shouldn't sin.

You gave us gifts:
talents and roles.
You gave us gifts,
to perfect our souls.

You gave us power to get wealth,
Your giving the example
You gave us power to get wealth,
giving in love: our preamble.

You gave our healing,
so sickness wouldn't reign.
You gave our healing;
we have Christ's bloodstain.

You gave us true love,
for us to receive.
You gave us true love,
none greater ever conceived

You are the GodMan, Jesus -
also known as, The Giver.

The Logos
John 1:1-3, 14; Hebrews 4:12

He spoke the Word
without a mouth;
The Word houses His power
and blueprint for creation
and reality was born

Creation was created
As the words spoken
discerned His heart and
accomplished His purpose

His Word is the wisdom
To fashion reality
That's not fully known
by man
For it transcends
commonsense
and current science

Thus, the magnificent
and exquisite -
galaxies,
species,
angels,
heaven & hell,
even the human mind -
sprang from the intelligence
housed in the Word

This Word is the Logos:
The Thinker
of the thought
of thought
this Logos
lived among us
as Jesus Christ
This Jesus is God

Uni-verse
Genesis 1:1

In the beginning...
Before spacetime came to be
there was nothing but God
but there were no eyes to see
Him

...God ...
Elohim - the One and True,
desired a family to love,
and He thought of you

...created the heaven...
His words discerned His intent,
and accomplished the things
for which they were sent.
Spacetime came to be,
and all expanse, all realities,
When His Word declared
"Let there be _____."

...and the earth.
still a mystery to an extent
with laws: legal, physical, spiritual
though man's exploring won't relent.

One God, Who spoke
One Word or verses
Yielding one "verse":
The Uni-verse

31

There, At The Cross

Obedience took Him there.
My sin hung Him there.
Isaiah 53:5
His love kept Him there,
John 3:16
Until death took Him from there.
He satisfied God's wrath there. (I John 4:10)

He crushed satan's head there. (Genesis 3:15; Mark 15:22)
He destroyed his works there. (I John 3:8)
He rendered him useless there. (Hebrews 2:14)
And His power conquered there.
An eternal victory was finished there. (John 19:30)

His blood was shed there.
It purged my conscience there. (Hebrews 9:14)
It bought my healing there. (Isaiah 53:5)
His death gave me life there.
He gave an object for my faith there.

God & man were reconciled there. (II Corinthians 5:19)
For the blood was applied there.
The Way was made there.
The truth was spoken there.
And in death, *The life* was birthed there. (John 14:6)

There,
at the CROSS!

Life
John 14:6; John 17:3; Proverbs 20:27

what is life?
is it security of money?
is it the allure of worldly power?
is it status and prestige with men?
is it lusts for the opposite sex?

Who is Life?
is He not security when vulnerable?
is He not the certainty of supernatural power?
is He not status and prestige with God?
is He not better than husband or wife?

While life for fallen mankind
likely consists solely of
money, power, prestige, and sex,
life for the saint revolves around
One:
JESUS Christ.
He is our Life.

For truly without Him
men are dead men breathing -
existing, yet not alive
walking, yet going nowhere
ever learning,
but never coming to the knowledge of the Truth…

until He Who is Truth - Jesus -
saves us, takes up abode within us,

lighting our new candle
a metamorphosis
once a sinner, now a saint.

now, with Him,
saints are living men breathing
existing, and alive
walking, and moving onward to glory
ever learning, and being led into ALL TRUTH

so
don't be content to merely exist
instead
receive eternal Life
in Jesus Christ!

The Living Tabernacle
Exodus 26:31-37; Matthew 1:23

The tabernacle of Moses
housed: the Holy Place,
and the Most Holy Place,
the mercy seat,
the commandments,
Aaron's rod with buds,
the ark of the testimony,
the lampstand,
the altar of incense &
the table for the bread.

That was then…
Only shadows of
what was to come,
or rather
Who was to come.

For now we have Emmanuel
God with us
The living Tabernacle

Instead of a seat,
We have One full of mercy

Instead of 10 commands,

We have Him Who fulfilled the Law

Instead of Aaron's rod,
We have Him with all authority

Instead of light that will dim,
We have the eternal Light of the World

Instead of smoke from incense,
We have Him Who answers prayer

Instead of bread that rots,
We have the Word of God from heaven

Instead of one passing through a veil,
We all have The Way: unimpeded access to Him

Who is this figure?
Who embodies
all that the tabernacle represents
and so much more?
None other than
The GodMan:
The Lord Jesus Christ of Nazareth
Who tabernacled among us
And through His blood
can live in us!

The Revealed One
Hebrews 1:1-3; John 1:1-4, 14

First, He spoke to Adam
Then He made a covenant with Abraham.
He revealed promise of prophecy
to the fathers thereafter
and to the kings of the Hebrews
usually by His prophets.

But none of these insights
excelled the prophecies
concerning the Revealed One:
The root and offspring of David;
Likened to Moses,
But superior to him
And to the angels
Forever our Great High Priest.

For this One
Is the Revealed One:

after the flesh, son of Joseph,
after the Spirit, Son of God;

after the flesh, Rabbi of wisdom,
after the Spirit, The Wisdom of God;

after the flesh, a carpenter,
after the Spirit, The Maker of all things;

after the flesh, dead at 33,

after the Spirit, eternal;

after the flesh, a speaker of His Word,
after the Spirit, The Word of God.

Who is this One?
Jesus Christ -
the last revelation of God
to mankind.
Now, saints merely reveal
the Revealed One.
For there is nothing new,
after His Son.

The Glue Guy
Hebrews 1:3; Colossians 1:17

What holds all things?
From the atom and its proton
To the flying flock who sing
Heralding the morn in song

Who holds all things?
From constellations
To Saturn and its rings
To nerves and their sensations

Who keeps the planets
In perfect orbit
      Sustaining life on earth
Changing a few degrees
Either way leads to death
      Concerning habitats - a dearth
Or Who keeps man's mind
A complex system that runs neurons
      Epochs cannot tell its worth
Who conceived mankind
Miraculous mixing of earthly and divine
      Filling new moms with mirth

Who hath shed forth all of this?
With the word "be"
No details did He miss

Like the athlete
who is essential

to his team's success
Jesus is the Glue Guy
Holding all things together
Upon Him and His Word
All things rest!

Indefatigable Incarnation
Luke 1:35; John 10:17-18

Venit.
He came...
Born of a virgin
As God Who became man
Eternal Spirit wrapped in flesh
Anointed One Who is smeared
Fulfillment of ancient prophecy
In learning God's will: tireless

Mortuus est.
He died...
Betrayed by His friend
Abandoned by disciples
Flogged by Romans
Cursed & nailed to a tree
Bearing our sins and infirmities
In doing God's will: Tireless

Resurrexit.
He rose…
Robbed the grave
Delivered the righteous dead
Appeared to His followers
Giving substance to our faith
Authoring our salvation
In finishing God's will: TIRELESS

The One of Whom i speak
is Jesus Christ:

the indefatigable incarnation!

Part II:

JESUS IN US

New Skins, New Wine
Mark 2:22; Luke 5:37-38; Matthew 9:17

Pour Your Spirit into me.
New Wine: I taste and see.
Shackles cannot bind. I'm free!

Pour Your Spirit into mine.
Fill my new skin, this new spirit abides
within, from where Yours shines

Pour Your Spirit on us.
Drunken with new Wine, thus
we've enough power to thrust
Satan's gate to the dust.
His eternal defeat is a must.
Let his weapons decay and rust,
Every lie, every evil lust.
Pour Your Spirit on us.

For Your Spirit is the new Wine.

Only new wineskins, my new spirit,
can hold:
in with the new, out with the old.
It houses the Infinite One, riches untold

New skins for new Wine

(Re)wired
Romans 12:1-2; Ephesians 4:23

Neuron-to-neuron-to-neuron
messages are sent this way,
in your brain,
which is the hardware
driven by your mind,
which is the software.

Every thought pattern -
even sinful ones -
creates a neuro-pathway.
Thus, these thoughts
yield behaviors which can repeat
like the worst virus.

Every time we engage
sinful thought patterns
we strengthen these neuro-pathways.
The sin becomes more entrenched,
Even a malignant virus,
Altering our software..

This is how the brain is wired

But thanks be to God!
Who always causes us to triumph!
For through creating action with verbs
And through employing
spiritual weapons -
Praise, worship, faith,

binding/loosing,
The name of Jesus, &
The blood of Jesus -
We create new neuro-pathways,
tied to holy behavior,
dismantle viral strongholds
thus, renewing our minds
to the deliverance of our souls
from the presence of sin.

This is how the brain is rewired!

Bear My Cross
Mark 8:34; Luke 9:23

Because i love Jesus
Myself i do deny
He's not just to please us
Or to catch the tears we cry

Yes, from us God desires more
His cross exposes us to His death
We die too - this is what's in store
Our lives an offering, not a theft

For He gave His life
So through this act He might restore
All who would escape the strife,
sin, and death we once bore

In our flesh and soul

So i tell Him,
"What a sacrifice of love!
You are faithful; You are true.
So the cross belongs to me,
And my heart belongs to You!

i give You access to all of me,
Yet a small gesture.
For You took my penalty,
As they stripped Your vesture.

i bear my light cross as i wait for my crown

i'll tell the world of the Treasure i've found."

POWER, Part II

Power within
Power over sin
Power without
To conquer satan's doubt

Power of His Spirit
Housed in mine
Brand new; i tap in, & feel it
Both sublime & divine

Power so great
He transcends description
Through Him
i defeat all opposition
Please believe, it's not fiction

Power of living Fire
That lights my new candle
Bringing satan ire -
The Spirit he can't handle
Or resist
Once i partake
Satan must cease and desist

Power of God
It's real
And can dwell in you
Please repent, dear friend
That's what you must do!

Dark Then Light
Genesis 1:2-3

The earth became dark
All was amiss
The devolution was stark
Because He took the *risk*

Then Light came forth
From the Words of His *mouth*
Without matter, it burst forth
All darkness fled south

My heart was dark
Its desires amiss
Always missed the mark
More vile than the Sith

But the parting of His *lips*
spoke Light to my soul
The Word cancelled my trip
To the depths of Sheol

Out of nothing good in me
He has recreated something new
Holy, pure, and free
Light has fallen, like fresh dew

For when His Words called for Light
It came to the earth
And within my soul, dark as night
Yet He shed Light to esteem my worth

Once, i was dark
Now i emit the Light
Thank You, Jesus!

Glory To Glory
II Corinthians 3:18

Look at My glory,
and be changed.
Let that be your story,
even through the pain.

Look at My glory,
and be changed.
Till your head is hoary,
much wisdom you've gained.

Look at My glory,
and be changed.
Progression to another glory,
you've become the same.

Look at My glory,
and be changed.
Once a whore
Now a *one-Man dame.*

For as the wife
Is the glory of her man   I Corinthians 11:7
So is Jesus' Bride - the Church -   Revelation 21:2-3, 9
The glory of the God-Man
Jesus.
As this wife gazes
At the glory of her Man,
She becomes more and more
like unto

The glory staring at her.

Until the day
Of consumma-
tion

From glory to glory

Ascend

God says,
"Ascend My dear son.
Grow in wisdom.
My victory you've won.

Ascend, My dear son.
Progress in knowledge.
Death you've overcome.

Ascend, My dear son.
Mirror My behavior.
Sin's power is done.

Ascend, My dear child.
Reflect My perfection.
Cause Me to smile.

Ascend, My dear child.
Rise like a god   John 10:34-35
Live forever, how wild!

Ascend, My dear child.
Prove the true Word,
That you are reconciled.

Ascend.
Return to your first state.
Then arise above that;
Be the greatest of the great."

<u>My Story Continues…</u>
Genesis 50:20; Romans 8:28

Despite trial after trial
When i thought i'd ever be senile
And that i couldn't go another mile
My story continues…

Despite the enemy's deception
A weapon formed, met with my reception
Seduction which blocked my spiritual perception
My story continues…

Despite my own ignorant errors
Driven by the effects of sin, a terror
Will i fall into the same trap? NEVER
My story continues…

Despite toiling for over ten years
Little work or no work, bringing me to tears
the one meant to love me leading the jeers
My story continues…

Despite Satan's lie that i would never minister
A lie from one who fathers all things sinister
Now i test all spirits, becoming a great inquisitor
My story continues…

My God has drawn good for me
From ALL these things -
Sins included.
Everything from His judgments

To His mercy and grace
To my brokenness
And subsequent humility
They have all been to my benefit
Tough love
From a tough God
It's forging a character within me
Beyond reproach
Propelling me into my destiny

But,
Jesus is not done with me yet!
MY STORY CONTINUES...

Payday

Revelation 19:11-16, 20-21; Revelation 21:1-27;
Revelation 22:1-5

Where i'll be paid for my work
Where i will no longer hurt

Where my tears will be gone
Where i'll sing a new song

Where i'll have a new name
Where He will have the same

Where i'll worship all day
Where it's daytime always

Where my striving will be done
Where my eyes will behold the Son

Where i'll get a divine mansion
Where my mind will undergo expansion

Where my pain will run away
Where, indeed, it can not stay

Where i'll enter one of twelve gates
Where my desires He'll satiate

Where the river of life flows
Where the tree of life grows

Where its leaves somehow heal the nations

Where believers will be paid for their patience

Where time will come to an end
Where, with Christ, eternity I'll spend

Where i'll reign with God forever
Where our bond none can sever

This Day is payday!
Thank God for heaven.

Restored
Romans 5:12-21

Adam and all who'd follow
Were meant to live
And in sin never wallow
But to God we'd give...

our lives would embody bliss
Of God we'd grasp more and more
No idols would we kiss
Recreating Eden throughout scores...

of cities covering the earth
Instead we fell
for he didn't value His worth
All we did forfeit, i cannot tell...

Of what we *gained*, i can -
Sin, death, and regression
This was NOT His plan
For He wanted royal succession...

For Adam, but instead
Death reigned over our kind
From the babe to the hoary head
But He had better in mind...

For the sons of men
To return as sons of God
As Moses did pen
The Seed of her would plod...

Trampling the enemy of our souls
But this was only prophecy
At the time, so waiting was our role
thus, there was no stopping he…

Who is death
Which worked in us through sin
Not simply taking our last breath
But devolution of all within…

Us: our bodies, spirits, and minds
A far cry from His aim
We left Eden behind
No global garden and many insane...

men in this planet
Who lead with arms
War after war: they plan it
Placing all in harms…

way, but after generations of futility
Came Christ with the ability
To establish godly stability
A perpetual end to hostility
For men with sin as a proclivity

His Spirit came; the upper room was first
Then He got in the worst
Saul, who was a curse
Went by Paul, writing to churches
In letters becoming Bible verses

The restoration has begun
He declared His church has won
The battle versus Satan
A war won without guns
For once again God can have sons...

and daughters, His kin
Armed with His Spirit within
Breaking the power of sin
Now death cannot win

The restoration of life
There's an end to all strife
Between God and His wife:
We've traversed from death to life

The restoration was His plan
It unfolds, now we stand
Regaining what Adam lost -
        Relationship, power, insight - we can
Be poised to cover the land
With Gospel words like grains of sand...

Too many to count; one for every ear
It transforms all who'll hear
inside out: our consciences clear
Renewing all we hold dear -
Spirit and soul - as we perfect fear
Of Jesus, Who surpasses any seer

And what's more?

New heaven, earth, and men who roar   Proverbs 28:1
Please obey His Word, I implore   Acts 2:38-39
And you too will be restored!

Joy

Joy can be found
In doing His will
That your life plays a sound
Reaching His holy hill

Joy can be found
By asking in Jesus' name
Our rejoicing resounds
A request granted is to blame (John 16:23-24)

Joy can be found
Even in the midst of pain
There's a gladness deep down
An oasis with rain

Joy can be found
When happy times leave
Depression tries to hound
Joy grants needed reprieve

Joy can be found
By receiving His own
His words won't hit the ground (Matthew 24:35)
His blessings aren't loans

Joy can be found
In the presence of God alone (Psalm 16:11)
You've searched all around
The truth is now shown!

Forever Friends
Proverbs 18:24; John 15:15

Jesus and i,
Together
Forever.
He in me
& i in Him
Never to part.

Jesus and i,
Together
Forever.
Perpetual friends,
A love exchange
With no end.

Jesus and i
Together
Forever,
A union
Of sweet
Communion.
I pray; He listens
And responds in turn,
Unveiling secrets,
Revelations remarkable,
Novel creativity,
Wisdom without bounds.

Jesus and i
Together

Forever.
From repentance,
Through this life -
With its ebbs and flows
Its vexation and victories -
to the catching away
And On
Into eternity.

Jesus and i...
Together
Forever
FRIENDS.

There's More
Hebrews 6:1-5; II Peter 1:1-4; II Corinthians 5:17

There's more...
You're a super-natural hybrid,
not *just* human
By their wonders and writings,
the Apostles have proven.

There's more...
In Him, you're a new kind,
Even of a new species,
Leaving the old behind.

There's more...
You are of a godly race,
His Spirit within your new spirit (Mark 2:22)
The Infinite housed in finite space.

There's more...
Your nature is now divine
With the power of God within
Your new tongues are the first sign.

There's more...
With sins you are no longer bound.
Possessing all you need to succeed,
Let your praise to Him resound.

There's more...
As you partake of His Spirit,
With Him yours is imbued.

It's godly; don't fear it.
Rather, dance around your pew!

There's more...
Just receive
Fully know this new you
Won't you believe?

Look On Jesus
Hebrews 12:2

Troubles surround you.
Pain in mind and body too,
Money short; bills are due,
What's a man to do?

Circumstances stand around,
Weapons that speak with no sounds.
Lift your eyes, which were down,
Much peace is then found.

While trials don't please us,
Seem to suffocate. Please just,
Let the Word seize us.
And LOOK ON JESUS!

Flood Me

Baptize me again, with
Spirit: life-giving flow
Wash over me
Wash over me

Pour out Your Spirit
Overflow my wineskin
Wash over me
Wash over me

Energize my soul
Give life to my spirit.
Wash over me
Wash over me

Purge my conscience
Grant me revelation
Wash over me
Wash over me

Commune with me
Mingle Your Spirit with mine
Wash over me
Wash over me

Infuse me
With Your raw glory
Wash over me
Wash over me

Spirit of God, flood me!

Soul & Spirit
Leviticus 17:11; Genesis 2:7

What is the soul,
but the mind, heart, and will?
What is the spirit,
but the conscience,
intuition,
and seat of fellowship
with God and men?

The life of the flesh is in the blood.
This life is your soul.
So your soul extends through your blood,
and through the blood it animates
every portion of your frame.

The product of
His breath
plus the jar of clay -
Adam's body -
yielded the living soul.

The life of the soul is the spirit.
The soul takes in spirit
with its every breath.
Through the spirit,
the soul pulls from the Life of God.

The life of man is his soul.
The life of his soul is his spirit.
Yet,

the Life of the spirit
is
God's Spirit.

Breathe in the Holy Spirit
And renew your spirit
To save your soul!

About The Author

Patrick Henry, M.A., M.A., LPC is a Chicago native and two-time graduate of Northwestern University, where he earned a bachelor's degree in Psychology and a master's degree in Counseling Psychology. Most recently, he earned another master's in Developmental Psychology from Loyola University Chicago. Patrick has written poetry for roughly 20 years, and he has written solely Christian pieces since shortly after Jesus saved him in 2002. From 2002-2017, he attended Christ Temple Apostolic Faith Church in Chicago, IL where he served as a teacher in Sunday School and in D.R. Bell Bible College and as a drummer. Patrick now attends Endtime Apostolic Christian Holiness Church under the pastorate of Bishop Dr. Derrick A. Reeves, Th.D, Ph.D., D.D.

In addition to being an author of Christian poetry and books, Patrick is a trained Christian counselor, Bible teacher, and preacher. He is founder/CEO/chief editor at 3P: PH Pentecostal Publishing, LLC. Patrick can be reached at 614-522-9624 or at pathen238@gmail.com.

Acknowledgements

I want to thank everyone/everything that made this book possible – family, friends, mentors, and my tests/trials. To not neglect anyone, I will avoid listing names. You all were used to help create experiences in my life that God used as "material" for this book. I love you all with the love of Jesus Christ! And finally, thank You Jesus for giving me this gift of writing and allowing me to share it with the world!

BONUS POEM

The Real Phoenix
Romans 6:4; Ephesians 5:30

Just as the mythical bird
Rose from death, how absurd
Speaking volumes, without one word
By this act it's sermon is heard

Just as it continually regenerates
It's fiery covering through space penetrates
A royal bird, not to be denigrated
Or to the effects of sin relegated

So is He: revived to live evermore
and...

So
am
i
Once a dead man dying
Whose whole life was a lie
Unable to produce good with many tries

But NOW
i too, in newness of life, have risen
Baptized in Spirit & fire, given...
To transform soul and body, no sinnin'
The old me done away, new life livin'

As i repent

i die and live again
Ever a saint in His Body
Born anew from within
through...

Jesus Christ: The Real Phoenix

www.ingramcontent.com/pod-product-compliance
Lightning Source LLC
Chambersburg PA
CBHW062027040426
42447CB00010B/2175